M000283860

I CANNOT
LIE BY YOUR FIRE

In Loving Memory of
Man's Best Friend

Robinson Jeffers
Illustrated by Nick Bland

SOUVENIR PRESS

I've changed my ways a little; I cannot now
    now
Run with you in the evenings along the
    shore,

Except in a kind of dream; and you, if
    you dream a moment,
You see me there.

So leave awhile the paw-marks on the
    front door
Where I used to scratch to go out or in,
And you'd soon open; leave on the
    kitchen floor
The marks of my drinking-pan.

I cannot lie by your fire as I used to do
On the warm stone,

Nor at the foot of your bed; no, all the
    nights through
I lie alone.

But your kind thought has laid me less than six feet
Outside your window where firelight so often plays,

And where you sit to read – and I fear
    often grieving for me
Every night your lamplight lies on my
    place.

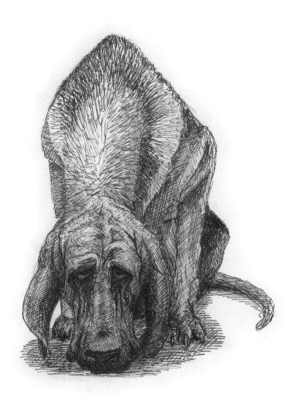

You, man and woman, live so long, it is hard
    hard
To think of you ever dying.
A little dog would get tired, living so
    long.

I hope that when you are lying
Under the ground like me your lives will
    appear
As good and joyful as mine.

No, dears, that's too much to hope: you
    are not so well cared for
As I have been.

And never have known the passionate undivided
Fidelities that I knew,

Your minds are perhaps too active, too
   many-sided. . . .
But to me you were true.

You were never masters, but friends. I was
    your friend.
I loved you well, and was loved. Deep
    love endures
To the end and far past the end. If this is
    my end,
I am not lonely. I am not afraid. I am still
    yours.

I Cannot Lie by Your Fire

I've changed my ways a little; I cannot now
Run with you in the evenings along the shore,
Except in a kind of dream; and you, if you dream
      a moment
You see me there.

So leave awhile the paw-marks on the front door
Where I used to scratch to go out or in,
And you'd soon open; leave on the kitchen floor
The marks of my drinking-pan.

I cannot lie by your fire as I used to do
On the warm stone,
Nor at the foot of your bed; no, all the nights
      through
I lie alone.

But your kind thought has laid me less than six feet
Outside your window where firelight so often
      plays,
And where you sit to read – and I fear often
      grieving for me
Every night your lamplight lies on my place.

You, man and woman, live so long, it is hard
To think of you ever dying.
A little dog would get tired, living so long.
I hope that when you are lying

Under the ground like me your lives will appear
As good and joyful as mine.
No, dears, that's too much hope: you are not so
    well cared for
As I have been.

And never have known the passionate undivided
Fidelities that I knew,
Your minds are perhaps too active, too many-
    sided. . . .
But to me you were true.

You were never masters, but friends. I was your
    friend.
I loved you well, and was loved. Deep love endures
To the end and far past the end. If this is my end,
I am not lonely, I am not afraid. I am still yours.

Robinson Jeffers – American poet, d.1962 aged 75.

If you need someone to talk to about your loss ...

United Kingdom
The Pet Loss Befrienders Service:
0800 0966606

This special gift edition first published 2001 by Souvenir Press Ltd
43 Great Russell Street, London WC1B 3PD

Reprinted 2003, 2004

© 2001 Souvenir Press Ltd and is published by arrangement with Randon House Trade Publishing, a division of Random House, Inc.

ISBN 0 285 63623 5

Printed in Singapore